CONTENTS

Parent and Caregiver Tips for Creating Nonfiction Readers

The high-interest topics in the ***Favorite Food Franchises*** series are sure to get your young reader excited about reading nonfiction. While exploring a fascinating subject, your reader will be introduced to new facts, ideas, and vocabulary.

Tips for Reading Nonfiction

Talk about Nonfiction

Explain that nonfiction books provide facts about real-world topics. When readers read nonfiction, they gain a rich understanding of the world. They build background knowledge that provides a foundation for learning and academic success.

Look at the Parts

This book contains the following helpful features. Share the purpose of each feature with your reader.

Photos, Captions, and Graphic Aids
The photos, captions, maps, diagrams, time lines, and other graphic aids in nonfiction texts contain a wealth of information. Help your reader identify different ways information can be displayed.

Sidebars
These extra tidbits of information help satisfy readers' curiosity and expand their knowledge.

Table of Contents
Located at the front of the book, this list shows the big ideas within the text and the page numbers where they can be found.

Glossary
Located at the back of the book, the glossary defines key words and phrases that are related to the topic. These words and phrases can be found in the text in colored type.

Comprehension Questions (Fact Check)
Multiple-choice questions help readers self-check to make sure they understand what they read.

Index
Located at the back of the book, the index is an alphabetical list of topics and the page numbers where they can be found.

With a little help and guidance, your reader will be on their way to enjoying and learning from nonfiction books.

Mitchell Lane
PUBLISHERS
mitchelllanepub.com

2001 SW 31st Avenue
Hallandale, FL 33009

First Edition, 2025.
Author: Laura Purdie Salas
Designer: Rhea Magaro
Editor: Kim Thompson

Series: Favorite Food Franchises
Title: Dunkin' / by Laura Purdie Salas

Hallandale, FL : Mitchell Lane Publishers, [2025]

Library bound ISBN: 979-8-89260-313-3
Paperback ISBN: 979-8-89260-435-2
eBook ISBN: 979-8-89260-319-5

PHOTO CREDITS
Alamy: Allen Creative/Steve Allen, cover, 1, 29; Freer Law, 4; ClassicStock, 8; Randy Duchaine, 10; Sipa USA, 23; Shutterstock: dwph, cover; MariaLev, 1; Kirkam, 3; rangizzz, 4, 9, 13, 15, 16, 20, 23, 24, 27; Surya S Nair, 5; Shaiith, 6; Ashley Hazel, 7; f11photo, 9; TrishaMcmillan, 9; Mashka, 13; Lucky Business, 14; Clari Massimiliano, 14; hedgehog94, 14; PixaHub, 15; Nataly Studio, 16; Maria Castellanos, 17; mattburchell, 18; rblfmr, 19; Tada Images, 19; Deutschlandreform, 20; Exzr, 21; Happy Author, 21; MVelishchuk, 22; Monkey Business Images, 23; Tinseltown, 24; Tada Images, 25; Moab Republic, 26; Jonathan Weiss, 26; rblfmr, 26; Triff, 26; ATIKAN PORNCHAIPRASIT, 27; Augustine Bin Jumat, 27; Mariia_A, 32

CHOCOLATE ICED GLAZED
DOUB CHOCOLAT
Celebrations
COCO CHOCO
SWEET Celebrations
CHOCO SPARK
SUGAR
SIGNATURE Treat
ORIGINAL GLAZED®
CHOCOLATE ICED GLAZED
SIGNATURE Treat
ORIGINAL GLAZED®

How do you know a donut's a donut? It's got a hole in the center! Bakers punch the middle out of each circle of dough before they fry it in hot oil. That way, the donut cooks evenly all the way through.

That center dough used to be wasted. But in 1973, Dunkin' Donuts started frying up those round bits of donut dough. They sold the donut holes as Munchkins®. Now, Dunkin' sells about one billion donut holes each year.

In the Beginning

William Rosenberg was the **founder** of Dunkin' Donuts. He opened a restaurant in Quincy, Massachusetts, in 1948. He called it Open Kettle. It sold donuts for a nickel and cups of coffee for a dime.

Customers sat on stools at the counter. The counter curved around like a question mark. A server could stand inside the curve and fill up everyone's coffee cup.

Do You Know Dunkin'?

Quincy, Massachusetts, is a suburb outside the large city of Boston, Massachusetts.

Rosenberg renamed his restaurant Dunkin' Donuts in 1950. Rumor says the name was inspired by the practice of dunking donuts into hot coffee.

That first Boston-area restaurant was a success. You can still visit it today. More than 75 years later, it is open for business.

Dunkin' Donuts kept growing. In 1954, it had five **franchises**. It grew to 100 restaurants by 1963. Today, there are more than 13,000 locations worldwide.

The Dunkin' Experience

It's easy to spot a Dunkin' restaurant. The bright, puffy, pink and orange letters on its logo almost look like plump donuts.

Order at the counter. Bright lighting makes it easy to see your choices. You can also order online or in the drive-thru. Then, take your treats to a clean white table.

Sometimes, Dunkin' is noisy. People grab coffee on their way to work. Kids beg their grown-ups for more donuts. Loud music and ads often play. Tune it all out and enjoy every bite.

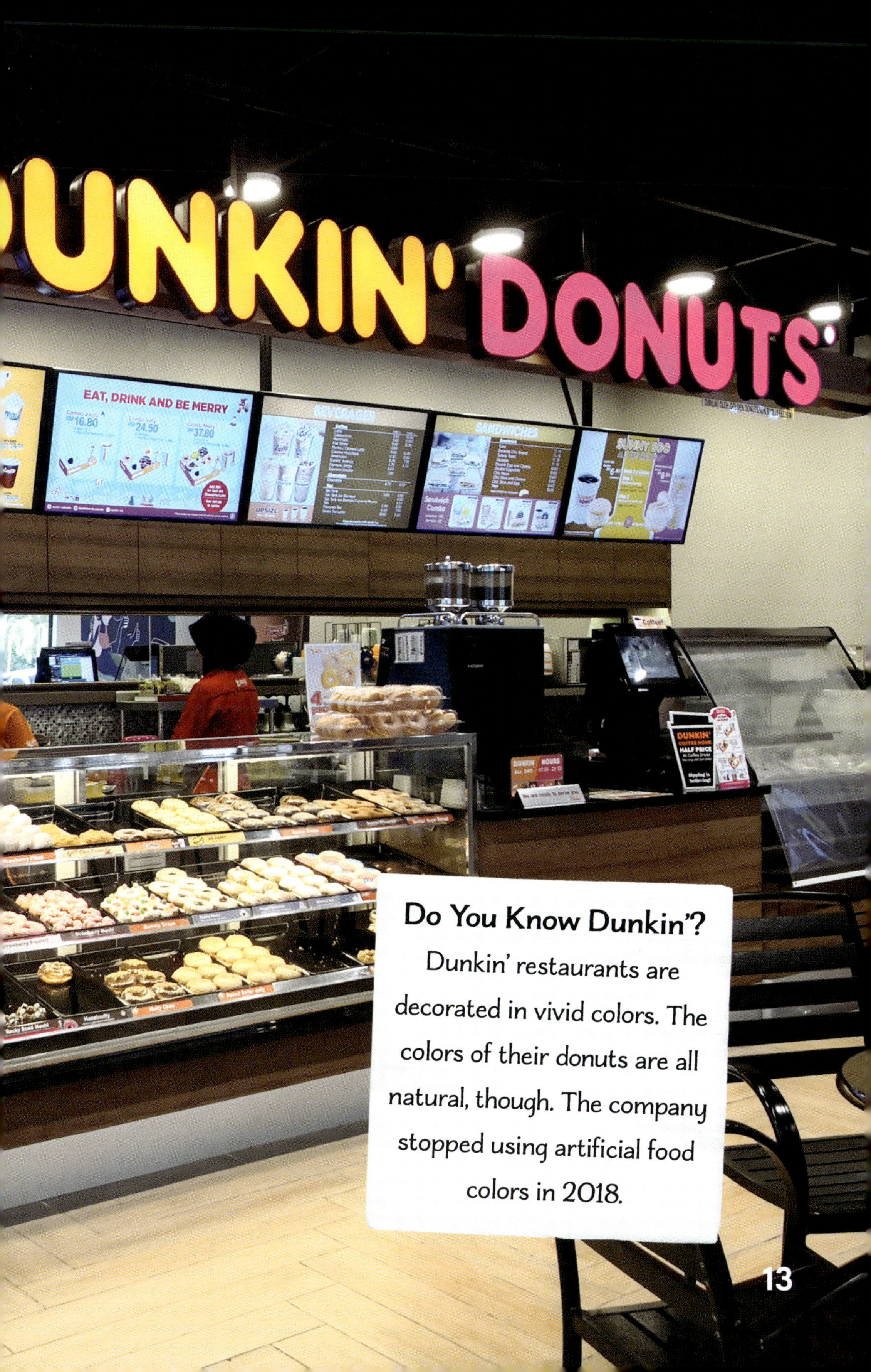

Do You Know Dunkin'?

Dunkin' restaurants are decorated in vivid colors. The colors of their donuts are all natural, though. The company stopped using artificial food colors in 2018.

DUNKIN' DONUTS
DD LATTE

Once, bakers at each location started making donuts before dawn. Today, Dunkin' stores still have the option of baking fresh donuts. Not many do.

Some franchises use a **central kitchen**. With this method, many stores chip in money to build and operate one big **facility**. Bakers work there each night. Fresh donuts get shipped out daily to each franchise.

Another method is having the Dunkin' company ship frozen donuts to a franchise. Workers finish baking them and add fillings and toppings.

Do You Know Dunkin'?

Dunkin' has been accused of using low-quality ingredients in some menu items, such as fake blueberries in its blueberry donuts.

WHAT'S ON THE MENU?

Dunkin' offers dozens of donut flavors. The fluffy glazed donut is airy with a sweet, crispy glaze. The coconut donut is coated with coconut flakes. The Boston Kreme donut has cream filling and chocolate icing on top.

Special donuts are available only at certain times of the year or in certain areas. A heart-shaped Valentine's Day donut has pink sprinkles. The Fenway Faithful and Inter Miami donuts honor local sports teams.

Do You Know Dunkin'?

Nutrition experts consider donuts to be a special treat, not an everyday snack. A Dunkin' glazed jelly stick contains 540 calories and 37 grams of sugar.

In addition to donuts, Dunkin' sells bagels, muffins, and other baked goods.

You can also order breakfast sandwiches. Workers add a **pre-cooked** egg and some cheese to a bagel, English muffin, or croissant. They add bacon, sausage, or turkey sausage. A quick trip to the oven results in a hot, tasty breakfast.

The company wants to be known for more than just donuts. In 2018, it even took *Donuts* out of its name. The business that became famous as Dunkin' Donuts switched to simply Dunkin'.

Do You Know Dunkin'?

Not everyone was happy about the name change. Some donut fans feared that Dunkin' would no longer sell their favorite treats. Some Boston-area customers felt that the company was being disloyal to its roots.

Recently, Dunkin' has shifted its focus toward coffee. It sells a variety of fancy coffee drinks. Other beverage choices are teas, fruit drinks, and smoothies. Customers can order from a secret menu of **concoctions** that combine different flavors.

SPREADING JOY

Dunkin' runs the Joy in Childhood Foundation. It has spent 49 million dollars to help bring happiness to sick kids and teens. The program provides dog visits and gaming equipment to hospitals. It puts on prom events so that teen patients can enjoy a special night.

DUNKIN'®
JOY
IN CHILDHOOD FOUNDATION

Do You Know Dunkin'?

Singer Noah Kahan performed at the University of Vermont Children's Hospital in 2023. Songs and donuts brought holiday cheer. It was one of many events that have been arranged and sponsored by Joy in Childhood.

Dunkin' Donuts' most famous "baker" was Fred. Actor Michael Vale played Fred in TV commercials from 1982 to 1997. The exhausted baker always said, "Time to make the donuts." He reminded people that Dunkin' Donuts were made fresh every single day.

Dunkin' introduced a new **slogan** in 2006. It's "America runs on Dunkin'." The catchphrase refers to coffee. Coffee has **caffeine**, and people drink it for energy. The advertising does not mention that too much caffeine is not good for you.

Do You Know Dunkin'?

Actors Ben Affleck, Matt Damon, and Jennifer Lopez have appeared in Dunkin' ads. So has former NFL quarterback Tom Brady. Many of these stars have a special connection to the city of Boston.

DUNKIN' DONUTS®
DRIVE THRU
LONG BEACH RUNS
ON DUNKIN'

Because Dunkin' started near Boston, it is still most popular in the eastern United States. However, there are more than 13,000 Dunkin' locations worldwide.

The Dunkin' company sold for more than 11 billion dollars in 2020. That's a lot of donut dough! The business continues to change and grow. What's next for Dunkin'? We'll have to watch and see. And enjoy a donut while we wait!

New York, NY

Chicago, IL

Indianapolis, IN

Singapore

Thailand

Do You Know Dunkin'?

Dunkin' is now owned by Inspire Brands. This huge company also owns Arby's, Buffalo Wild Wings, Jimmy John's, and more.

INSPIRE

A Dunkin' Time Line

1948 William Rosenberg starts a coffee and donut shop called Open Kettle near Boston, Massachusetts.

1950 Rosenberg changes his restaurant's name to Dunkin' Donuts.

1970 The first international Dunkin' Donuts opens in Japan.

1973 Donut holes called Munchkins are added to the menu.

1982 Fred the baker appears in his first television commercial. He makes the phrase "Time to make the donuts" famous.

2006 "America runs on Dunkin'" becomes Dunkin' Donuts' new slogan.

2018 Dunkin' Donuts drops *Donuts*. Its new name is simply Dunkin'.

2020 Inspire Brands buys Dunkin' Brands Group for more than 11 billion dollars.

2021 A bike-thru lane is added to a Dunkin' location in the Philippines.

DUNKIN'
DUNKIN'
DRIVE THRU
DUNKIN'

GLOSSARY

caffeine (ka-FEEN)
a chemical that acts as a stimulant on the body and that occurs naturally in some foods and drinks, such as coffee

central kitchen (SEN-truhl KICH-uhn)
a kitchen that makes food for several locations of a restaurant

concoctions (kuhn-KAHKT-shuhnz)
mixtures made by combining different ingredients

facility (fuh-SIL-i-tee)
a place or building designed for a particular activity

founder (FOUN-dur)
the person who starts a company or organization

franchises (fran-CHYE-sis)
individual locations of a chain store or restaurant; legal agreements that let people run businesses that sell products created by a larger company

glaze (glayz)
a liquid, usually sweet, that is used to form a coating on food

logo (LOH-goh)
a symbol that identifies a company

pre-cooked (pree-KUKD)
food that is cooked ahead of time and reheated when a customer orders it

slogan (SLOH-guhn)
a short phrase a company uses in its advertising

Fact Check

1. Dunkin' dropped *Donuts* from its name because it wants to be known for _____.
   A. tea B. sandwiches C. more than just donuts

2. The colors on Dunkin's logo are _____.
   A. black and white B. orange and pink
   C. dark brown and white

3. The Joy in Childhood program has a mission of helping kids who are _____.
   A. sick B. smart C. alone

4. Dunkin' is most popular in the _____ United States.
   A. western B. eastern C. southern

Answers: 1. C, 2. B, 3. A, 4. B

Further Reading

Atherton, David. *David Atherton's Baking Book for Kids: Delicious Recipes for Budding Bakers*. Somerville, MA: Candlewick, 2023.

Cohn, Jessica. *On the Job in a Restaurant*. South Egremont, MA: Red Chair Press, 2016.

Goldman, Duff. *Super Good Baking for Kids*. New York: HarperCollins, 2020.

On the Internet

Biz Kid$: Young Entrepreneur Profiles
https://bizkids.com/groups/profiles
Learn about young people who have started their own companies.

Food Network: Cooking with Kids
https://www.foodnetwork.com/recipes/packages/recipes-for-kids/cooking-with-kids
Find recipes from the network for fun in the kitchen.

King Arthur Baking Company: Instructional Video
https://www.kingarthurbaking.com/learn/bakeforgood
Learn to bake bread in this video just for kids.

INDEX

ABOUT THE AUTHOR

Laura Purdie Salas is an award-winning author who lives and writes in Minnesota. Her many books include poetry and nonfiction. Laura loves to read, play board games, knit, explore nature, and spend time with her husband and two daughters. She also eats way too much fast food! When Laura swings into a Dunkin', she usually gets a small bacon breakfast sandwich. Sometimes, she accidentally buys a chocolate-cream-filled donut. Visit Laura at laurasalas.com.